NOT INTO THE BLOSSOMS

AND NOT INTO THE AIR

Elizabeth Jacobson

Winner of the New Measure Poetry Prize

Parlor Press
Anderson, South Carolina
www.parlorpress.com

Parlor Press LLC, Anderson, South Carolina, 29621

Printed in the United States of America
S A N: 2 5 4 - 8 8 7 9

Library of Congress Cataloging-in-Publication Data on File

978-1-64317-028-2 (paperback)
978-1-64317-029-9 (PDF)
9978-1-64317-030-5 (ePub)

1 2 3 4 5

Cover design by David Blakesley.
Cover art: Joanne Kaufman, *Roses*, joannekaufman.com
Printed on acid-free paper.

Parlor Press, LLC is an independent publisher of scholarly and
trade titles in print and multimedia formats. This book is available
in paperback and ebook formats from Parlor Press on the World
Wide Web at http://www.parlorpress.com or through online and
brick-and-mortar bookstores. For submission information or to
find out about Parlor Press publications, write to Parlor Press,
3015 Brackenberry Drive, Anderson, South Carolina, 29621, or
email editor@parlorpress.com.

For David,
and for Willa and Oliver

Contents

Not into the Blossoms and Not into the Air

Still I feel the red in my mind…
—Emily Dickinson

I

All mountains walk with their toes on all waters and splash there
—Eihei Dogen

Birds Eating Cherries from the Very Old Tree

I thought I would make a short list of what is not a feeling.
Birds are not feelings.
Birds eating cherries from the tree are not feelings.
This is the best entertainment, I say to myself, *watching birds eating cherries*,
and now I have made a feeling.

The robin's beak glistens with the sticky juice.
When a cherry comes off a branch, snagged on the sharp point of its beak
the robin flies away with the cherry, perches on a fence post.
But the robin cannot eat the cherry if he is holding onto it,
so he drops it and goes back to the tree for more.
The robin is not a feeling.
The deep rust of the robin's breast is not a feeling.
But when I recognize the robin as male because of the color of his breast
a feeling about maleness swells from my center, and I shiver.

The magpies take big bites out of the cherries, half of one at once.
They squawk and scream at the other birds, who ignore them.
Listening to bird calls is not a feeling.
A very old tree is not a feeling.
But when I think of how very old the tree is, a feeling comes.

The magpies tug the cherries off the tree, sometimes 2 or 3 at a time.
They fly back to their nest and pull them apart like prey.
Below the nest piles of cherry pits lie in varying shades of decomposition.
A young sparrow flies from the cherry tree, giddy perhaps from all the sweetness,
and crashes into my window, breaking its neck.
The bird is warm in my hand.
And I have made another feeling.

The Cows

Now that I have read this story about the cows
I think of them at night when I cannot sleep,
how they are so still in their grassy field,
seemingly suspended like animations of themselves.
Even though there are only 3, I count them over and over,
envision them as if I were floating above their pasture,
observe the different stances they choose:
the 3 of them standing bottom to bottom, or
head to head,
sometimes in a row, one behind the other
sometimes side by side.
They stand where they want and nurse their calves.
They lie down in their field when they feel like it.
If the farmer wants to kill one, and it won't get in the truck
he gives up and lets it live.
If the farmer wants to sell one, and it won't get in the truck
he gives up and lets it stay.
I am glad I read this story by Lydia Davis.
I like to think of how she stood in her window and watched these cows.
I imagine how she may have moved from inside her house to outside her house,
depending on the weather, to stand and watch these cows,
month after month,
and although the details of their days are rather plain
she wrote a very essential story.
Right before I fall asleep I think about how there are no cows where I live
but there are mountains,
and I watch them move in this same way.
They open and close, depending on the weather
and like these 3 cows, these mountains are a few of the things left
that get to live exactly as they must.

I Always Know Where to Put My Hands on a Tree

I am outside at the plastic wicker table, under the coco palm
whose golf ball-sized seeds keep dropping on my paper
leaving wet brown spots from the sooty tropical mist,
trying to write a poem with the first line
I always know where to put my hands on a tree,
when a car goes by, mattress on the roof,
two guys in the front seats, each one with an arm out his window,
one hand on each side is all that's holding the mattress down
as they rush along with everyone else on the busy street.
A German shepherd that lives on the block,
sees a stray cat preening itself across the road,
yanks himself free from his person, dashes in front of the car
which jerks to a halt, mattress shooting off like a cannonball
flattening the biker who was crossing the road
and texting at the same time.
I always know where to put my hands on a tree,
tip of a branch in my mouth, flesh of its fruit on my lips.
The hog plums have fallen on the sand,
in the shadow of their own canopy.
Today is everyone's lucky day! The biker is young and sturdy,
her bike remains undamaged.
The men jump out of the car, yelling at the dog in Italian
calling to the girl, *Bella Bella,* as she speeds away,
stuffing her phone in her back pocket.
They chase after the dog, and when they catch it,
bring him back to his person
who pretends to smack him on the muzzle with the leash.
I always know where to put my hands on a tree,
this one here, tamarind pods open and sticky, their paste
not sweet, but bursting with sugar just the same.
I had been thinking of ending my poem by trying to explain
the smell that comes off the sea
as the sun is rising over it first thing in the morning,
how this heats the water which creates
a fragrant salty vapor which mixes with the air,

and that when I open my kitchen window while brewing my coffee,
intoxicates me so,
I get this tantalizing feeling
of being, this moment, in the exact right place.
I always know where to put my hands on myself,
like this, sun rising, salt air warming,
the sea inside me the tragedy of the living.

Next to You, Permanence

I wrapped the corpse of a juvenile bull snake I found on the road
around a slender branch of a young aspen tree,
coiling it into three even loops. The fluid
from the snake's body collected in its head,
which swelled to many times its normal size.
The next day, flies covered the body so thickly
I could not tell a snake was what they clung to.
On the third day, the snake hung like jerky from its branch,
the coils undone,
the skin split in places where delicate white bones pushed through.
This is what I was hoping for,
skin dropping away without a scent,
a helix of bones to set on my desk,
next to phantasms of you.
On the fourth day, when the snake began to move,
bulges under its desiccated skin rippled
like small hearts toward a new home
and I saw what was dead about the snake
had become the maggots of new life—
that the span from a seed, to the echo of what does
not change— is unbearable.

Dear Basho,

Thank you for sending your new poems.
I have a question.

But first I want to tell you I traveled North by bus the other day
to watch the pueblo dances, and there was a man on a high pole.
He had a dead lamb with him, whose neck had been slit.
The pole was a hundred feet in the air, and he leapt and twirled
on a small platform, which wobbled with his movements.
You would have liked to have seen his body, covered in sweat,
shimmering in the sun like a thousand yellow leaves.

That night I dreamt I was in a park of tall leafy trees
in various shades of autumn. I had a baby boy
in a backpack slung from my shoulders,
when out of nowhere appeared an enormous snake,
and in one wide bite it ate the baby off my back.

I woke with the morning light,
sweat pooling in the hollow between my collarbones.
            Basho, what is the world if it is not this uneasy faith
            puddling and drying as we thrust ourselves toward the sky?

You have been dead over three hundred years,
      but I feel you, Basho,
the length of your back, its weight across pine when you lie down.
Your knobby right hand, a stylus between your fingers.
                        I feel the way you feel yourself,
so many brown and silvering leaves,
each atop or underneath another.

Mountains Hidden in Mountains

Always my right side tugging me on,
                my right eye weeping,
                        the furious liver, shouting.

Always a rising,
    a mountain inside a mountain.
                    Always an uproar
           above the mountain.

The full moon
        pulling everything through.

Always the vacancy.

I promised to be naked,
            to walk on my knees up the mountain
                and if the mountain doubts me,
                I promise to take more off.

Unyielding Splat

after Gertrude Stein

No reasons and no momentariness's; no reasons but how is my tongue caught in your mouth? A pregnant armadillo, a briefcase of soft brown leather, there is something else under this hammock of red cedar and live oak, reason being the cause of my great size to appear all at once on this side of the window and then Ionic, this means burnt sienna, means magenta, a slender breast and no paperwork, this means monism, a premontane, a carcass.

Which Yellow Bird

Just to the right of the lifeguard shack,
a couple was fucking on a *chaise longue*

in the first row of many rows of chairs
which had been set up on the beach

in front of the Paradise Hotel.
A few feet away, sisters in matching gingham

piled shovels of sand on their mother's legs
as she lay on her stomach reading French *Vogue*,

sunning her shapely bottom,
while this couple went on fucking,

despite the foot traffic and the hustling cocktail servers,
despite the families with Kadima paddles,

their pink rubber balls
rolling toward the ocean.

The woman had pulled her swimsuit to one side,
and the man's trunks down just enough

so that as she straddled him
gyrating her hips slowly,

she gave him such pleasure
that his upper lip curled oddly toward his fleshy nose,

and his low moaning caused a Chihuahua tied to the pole of an umbrella
to yip.

Their plastic wine glasses and lunch plates had tipped off the chair,
and as I watched a small frenzy of gulls fight over the remains

of tuna sashimi and mango salad
I didn't have the nerve to turn away.

The towel that was covering the thin strip of her skin
where she joined herself to him

moved enough for me to see
she had a poem tattooed in Spanish,

just above her bikini line,
one phrase of Neruda

from *The Book of Questions*
and as she arched back

the poem opened
and I read

¿Cuál pájaro amarillo?

On the Island of Koshima

A young macaque wiped sand off his purple sweet potato before eating it.

Other monkeys watched him, side-eyed, while they ate sandy purple potatoes, and spit out the grit.

Soon many macaques were cleaning their potatoes.
Then all the macaques on the island were cleaning.

And then all macaques on all islands were cleaning.

One macaque washed a potato in the sea,
which gave it a pleasant salty taste.

And then all the macaques were washing potatoes in the sea,
leaving purple refuse on the beach,

which the seagulls began to pick up in their beaks,
dropping them back onto the sand.

Soon one seagull picked up a purple scrap, let it fall into the sea,
dove for it and ate it,

while minnows sped to catch the morsels.

Blood Moon

echoes of a hate crime

People are made of paper, love affairs,

   anything that tears easily.

A pregnant woman stands under the lunar eclipse,

   carves a swirl into a tree,

her baby is born with this same mark on his thigh.

It's just like the earth to come between the sun and the moon

   and cause this kind of mystery.

Point at a rainbow, and it will plummet and slice your finger off.

Use your lips instead, to show others what you are looking at.

Don't stand on high rocks or they will push you into the sky,

   and you will be pressed like a flower in a book.

People are made from rain showers, hatred, smears of spit,

   anything that might evaporate instantly.

That night, the moon was a true blood red,

not the pale rust of this moon, this morning.

   An entire human body coated red with blood,

   except where a path of tears washed through.

Don't stare at the moon

   or it will follow you persistently like a stray cat you have fed.

Don't hold out your hands when the sun is shining,

or you will burn continually with possibility.

People are made of buckets of sand, sequins of clay, desire,

anything that washes away easily.

Don't inhale too deeply, the scent of fallen leaves

pasted to the forest floor after a fresh rain,

or you will be repeatedly stepped on.

Don't count the seeds in a mound of bear scat

or just as many clouds will split open above your head.

Perfectly Made

Northern Flicker you woke me from dark sleep, your head
slammed into my window, neck snapped as you dropped
to the frozen ground. I had been dreaming of Gettysburg,
can you imagine? O*ur fathers brought forth a new nation,
conceived in liberty, and dedicated to the proposition that all* people *are created equa*
So perfectly made, I put my nail between the split of your beak, pulled
out the long worm of your tongue as if it were a measuring tape
coming out of its case, let go and watched it coil back, then my fingers
in your spotted under-down, a marvel, so warm,
so warm, in the bitter morning; I felt history
toying with itself as I stretched your stiffening wings
as far as they would spread and plucked out the stunning
bright orange tail feathers, one after the next, each quill spilling
a black ichorous ink onto my palms.

Each Day Travelling

Hello Buson!

I found another dead snake on the road today
and thought of you, the way you said, *Use the commonplace*

to escape the commonplace. Your square face
framed many canvases— the ashen leaves of cold days,

one purple thistle poking through.

You walked a long way
with pebbles in your shoes,

sat above a mountain pond considering your reflection
until nothing remained.

Here, the foothills are full of coyotes,
and in my room I am surrounded

with the yelps of their longing.
The senses flood; the sunken islands of brackish grass

appear to float in the pond—
                                        the whole world is in me,

an unrelenting grief that is each day travelling
so quickly into the next. How closely

you looked at things: *Struck by a raindrop, snail closes up.*
And then, dear Buson, and then?

You would have kissed me, I think,
on all sides of my face.

On Foot

I was staying at a farmhouse with no doors on the door openings, no windows on the window openings. Every night I slid a dresser behind the curtains hanging in the bedroom door frame, then rolled the heavy oil filled space heater behind that.

This was near the Rio Grande Gorge Bridge, and most days I went to stand on the pedestrian walkway. Crisis hotline boxes had been installed at every pylon with signs: *There Is Hope Make The Call.* Underneath the signs were big red buttons which lit up at night. It is tempting to push a big red button when you see one! I put my fingertip on it and circled the circumference. At the Gorge Bridge, the barrier is low and it would be easy to hop up on a cross rail and dive over. I thought of my friend who wrote a poem about standing at the spot on the famous bridge in Minneapolis where a celebrated poet had leapt into the Mississippi. When I travel a bridge on foot, I always consider jumping, even if it is a low bridge and I simply want to cool my feet.

I know two individuals who jumped from the Gorge Bridge. One was a friend of a friend who left a note saying he could not find another way up. The other, a seventeen-year-old, called his mother from the bridge to tell her he was going to jump. He waited the two hours it took for her to drive there, and as she ran pleading from her car, he leapt. Now she is trying to get the county to raise the railings, but I don't see how it matters. Anyone can walk to the rocky ledge of the gorge and soar into the ravine.

Getting back into the car, I remembered what my friend told me about that poet who dove to his death from the Minneapolis bridge. At the instant of his descent, he caught the eye of someone driving by, and he smiled, and he waved.

Blue Reminds Me of the Truth

Many of us find dead birds in our yards or on the street,
spread their wings with our fingers, bury them under a tree.
Yesterday I found a blue jay on US 1 that had been hit by a car
        mid-flight,
its black needle tongue suspended in shock,
feet curled as if still gripping a small branch.
I sped past it on my bicycle, then turned around to photograph it.
Later, I looked at the pictures and noticed how in death
the feathers on top of its head had turned from blue to gray.
Blue jays are unmistakable backyard birds for the blue and black
geometric markings on their wings. During courtship,
the male will often feed the female, but not always.

I am waiting in the shade under a live oak for my friend
who I haven't seen in 20 years, to take me to the beach.
She and I used to sleep together when we were 18, at her parent's house,
in the double bed with the frilly dust ruffle— her walls painted powder
        blue,
a Def Leppard poster taped above the headboard.
One night, she moved her hand across my stomach, between my legs,
and then when I did it to her
I came for the first time with another person.

There is no reason that blue should remind me of the truth,
but when I stand by the ocean,
or see a mountain in the distance as the sun is rising or setting,
giving the mountain a reflection of blueness,
I am sure there is something other than desire keeping me alive.

Violets

I dreamed I was a builder of bridges
and every bridge I built was made of vertebrae,
vertebrae linked to other vertebrae,
strung across mountain valleys like garlands
with violets sprouting in random places amid the bones.

Feeling the firm ground under your feet
while you are standing
is one of the great pleasures of having a body.
Or to be inside another person,
to have another person inside you.

People want the sweet taste,
like to know there is honey in the pot,
clear water in the pail.

But I didn't want that fullness,
or the purple flowers.
I only wanted to stand on the bones
with my arms raised toward the mist
and be completely free of mountains,
completely free of love.

II

I went out following the scented grasses
and returned chasing the falling blossoms

—Changsha

Curator of Insects

I started asking questions about how human bodies held together.
Already I was a certain age,

and not seeing any usual patterns.
My mind had become fuzzier,

mirroring the now fuzzier vision of my eyes.
I read about hymenoptera vision,

how paper wasps and honeybees
can remember the characteristics of a human face.

And since a dragonfly had remembered me,
I knew that this is true for them as well.

Some insects live only a few hours
or a few weeks,

30 days for a fruit fly,
2 months for a horse fly.

I saw the age of the body
might never again match the stretch of its will,

and like Keats, who remarked on the fading animation of his hand
at the end of his life,

there grew a sadness for this former vivacity,
yet unlike Keats, I had joy in its release.

Some of the things I do seem to move backwards.
Others feel as if they have a spherical momentum.

As I grow older, it all appears to taper,
yet there is also a broadening,

and although this is illogical,
this is what happens to people.

The dropping away leaves space,
which quickly floods with small things

like the blue-eyed dragonfly in flight,
facing me in the early morning,

or saving an ant from drowning
in a puddle of warm rainwater.

I cultivate flowers and trees for a small variety of bees,
offer them aspen and willow for when they are ailing.

They scrape the resin off the leaves
and secure it to their back legs.

A box elder bug has been resting on the base of the desk lamp for days,
his tender black limbs secured around the cord.

He is close to death, and waiting.
All my life, I tell him, *I have been told I should not see the things I see,*

the way I see them.
It is too late for all that now.

He turns his head and thorax toward my voice,
his opaque bead eyes red with inquiry.

> *"All the time I pray to Buddha I*
> *keep on killing mosquitoes."*
>
> —Issa

Issa, I killed 8 gophers this fall, held
each cold body in my open palm,

stroking the river colored fur between their silent black eyes
before dropping them into a plastic bag.

Their little hands were cupped
as if in death they cradled one last thing

because nothing does not continually hold
all of what remains, or all of what

has been carried somewhere else.
The tunnels these creatures dug in my yard,

destroying even the hardiest plants,
will soon be used by voles and rats,

and other gophers,
from other yards, that will be trapped and killed, by me.

I met a man who hunts elk.
He shot a large buck, and when he was beginning to dress it,

just as he made the first cut with his blade through the buck's neck,
this man opened his mouth to yawn.

The neck of the elk exploded, and the cervical fluid
burst from its spine,

infecting the man
with a parasite that nearly killed him.

Issa, I cannot absolve myself,
cannot clear impurities from my body.

You said, *A bath when you're born,*
a bath when you die,

how stupid.
How extraordinary.

Enter Here

You know, don't you, as creatures of breath,
our only nature is to die?

Rock changes shape,
moves to a new place,

stays there indefinitely, does not
long for something never quite enough.

A hard shiny knob
embedded in the dog's thick hide,

stretched the skin transparent.
I could see the insect turning around

inside its fluid-filled bubble.
I squeezed and squeezed until the knob

emitted a botfly with fully formed wings,
leaving a small exit hole in the dog's side.

Who can make a solid home in the body
enough? Find the steadiness of mountain

in flesh? When I turned and grabbed a cloth,
to wipe the wound clean,

my dog ate the fly.

14 Love Songs

Above a pond, I sit on a wooden bench
and throw pebbles into the willows.

A rush of sunlight and wind creates a path in a channel of water, dances
between the melting ice and brown islands of bulrush.

The resident osprey, its eyes the color of yellow grass,
follows my tossing hand.

Love is a diorama of inner life in an outer world.

I look down and find a chunk of fossilized rock
with an entire Paleozoic shell sticking out.

I am not afraid of love, but terrified of how it is my steady guide.

Once, when tired, I wandered off the trail and crawled under a tree to rest.

I woke to a young brown bear licking my boot.
Nothing had ever felt that good.

When I say I love you, what I mean is I wouldn't leave you.

Even if love is not loved back it doesn't go away,
although it may become a black hole.

Could this be what it's like for trees to lose the green from their leaves?

At noon the light shifts and the pond turns
into a mosaic of opaque green ice.

Orange carp rise in these cold watery chambers to breathe at the surface.

Always I am in love. Face to face with the sun. Face to face with the moon.

What Mates Midair:

after Sei Shonagon

Carpenter bees, wide as my lover's palm, navy in the ambient light of dusk. White throated swifts flying low in a river canyon. Box elder bugs end-to-end, all day long. Some species of hummingbirds. Garden slugs hanging from a strand of slime. Vines and lilies entwining through the pattern of my summer kimono. Dragonflies just touching down on my rakusu.

Just Like That

I found a triangular stone for you on the beach
and sent it in a letter.

It was smooth and worn where the persistent fingers of the ocean
worried perfect grooves in its surface

that your thumbs might have a place to rest and rub.
When I saw it on the wet sand, just as the foam rolled back,

I thought it was crushed bone, or the fin of a fish, and I
remembered your large hands,

how you cast them about when something useful is being said.
In the letter I tell you mourning doves

call *Hoo, Hoo— Hoo* from my tamarind tree,
the black bands at the back of their necks

open and close as the birds meet
the curiosities of the world,

their song a lament
for giving too much to what's ineffable,

and pulls us toward an internal edge.
When the letter came back, marked for insufficient postage

I went out for more stamps
and believe it or not, saw a woman get hit by a car.

Her body lifted up and flew over the traffic,
landing almost at my feet.

Her sturdy red leather clogs
remaining in the middle of the street.

Infinite Human Motion

They were killing flies at the Zen center.
Yellow strips of flypaper

hung like lanterns in various places around the zendo
until one of the visiting teachers complained,

and the residents took them down.
In honor of the fact this teacher was a Tibetan Buddhist,

the sticky mess was carried out back by the compost heap,
and chopped to pieces with a wood axe.

Once I saw an entire room filled with Calder mobiles.
Some were hung from the ceiling.

Others were on the floor, or on tables.
The ones floating down,

were almost touching
the ones reaching up.

The orange head of the cat in the *chat-mobile*
was bobbing at the wall,

while his black chest opened toward me.
A red nylon cord had been strung across the threshold,

for no one was permitted to enter this room
full of infinite human motion.

Last night, after seeing the film AWAKE, the Life
of Yogananda, a woman stood up from her seat and shouted,

I have a strand of Yogananda's hair in my locket!
Someone next to her shook her hand,

then someone else shouted,
Dragonflies are the insects of all six directions!

I closed my eyes
and counted these on my fingers.

Above, beyond, forward, side to side, and back, and below.

Common Octopus

I heard a scientist speak about new discoveries on multitasking.
Apparently, it is beneficial to multitask only when doing repetitive things
that are menial, like dishwashing, cooking, cleaning,
and taking care of babies, and not while doing something cerebral,
like reading a book or writing a poem.
He said that when you write a poem
you shouldn't be thinking about chewing roasted almonds
or swallowing hot or cold liquids,
or even what your next word might be.

Every day I walk by this parked school bus, and it drives me crazy
that the doors have been left wide open.
Any type of creature could get in and make a home,
gnaw the seats, leave deposits.
I went inside the bus to see what was going on, and so far nothing,
but tomorrow I will go back to check again,
try to wrestle the doors shut.

This same scientist said we should make lists on index cards,
one item per card, and then re-organize the cards to prioritize activities.
So many important things are being studied these days.
One day it is bonobos who are having the best sex on the planet,
and then the next day I read that the versatility of snake penises
provides the greatest pleasure for their mates.

I hear coffee is good for me and may prevent diabetes and Alzheimer's,
that it keeps inflammation at bay and my muscles from stiffening.
The next day I read coffee causes dehydration
and contains fungi and toxic mold, that these things may cause kidney failure.
I am told to drink 8 glasses of water a day, and then 16,
that I must drink so much water that as I gulp it down
it should pour straight out,
indicating my optimal level of daily consumption.
But then two days later I read too much water can kill me.

Yesterday a fourteen-year-old kid was arrested for building a clock from scratch
and bringing it to school to show his teacher.
They tossed him in jail and wouldn't allow him to call his parents
because they thought the clock was a bomb. Now, as compensation for this,
he is going to the White House to meet the President.

Much of the time when I am not writing poems
I am walking the roads looking for things to put in my poems.
The other day I met a man who was carrying a limp dog in his arms.
He said a car had hit her, and he had no other choice but to shoot her.
Now he was going to bury her by a small pond.
I think the man was in shock.
He was wearing a black leather holster which had fallen to his thighs
with shiny 45s in each side,
a cowboy hat stitched with sequins on his wide head.
My body quivered as I watched this man walk on.
Some trivial aches and pains in my right foot began to travel up to my brain
and I wondered if I should be drinking more coffee, or more water,
or less coffee or less water,
but mostly what I felt was pleasure in my body,
a thin veil of sensory impulses releasing over the outside of my skin.
I thought of the octopus vulgaris, how the female has a one-year lifespan.
During mating, the male inserts a tentacle into her,
his third tentacle to the left.
She hangs around her nest until the eggs hatch,
then she dissolves slowly over her spawn as they begin to swim around,
giving them her dying body to eat.

Ant Aubade

Each morning I wake
        and for a few moments
                there is perplexity,

        a kind of sorrow,
                for having left such pleasure behind.

From my window, a single black mammoth sunflower
        bent all the way over,
                touches its toes.

        To set it upright,
                I tape its high stalk
                to a thin plastic stake.
                      A lone ant searches the plant,
      ignores me as it stops to clean its antenna.

                Years ago I dreamed I grew a sunflower house,
a small square grassy plot bordered by tall, strong plants.

                    The hardy leaves of the stalks walled me in.
            The blooming heads nodded toward each other,
                offering shelter.
I could sit in it during a rainstorm without getting wet.

Nonetheless, I don't recall my dreams anymore.
        Such freedoms come these days
                          without asking.

Melancholia

Completely unsheathed, a frangipani
besides a fence, facing a river.
The fragility of bare finger-like tips.
The tender scaled boughs.
In the absence of leaves, leaves sprout forth.
In the absence of nectar, a sphinx moth
appears. *Frangipani.* Your aromatic selves,
when they bloom— each one
a love poem; each one a hoax.

Stridulation

Of course the cricket doesn't know
his liquid wave of sound has my mouth watering,
that I listen with concern
for the September evening when the humming will stop.
Will each little man who strums the brush and comb set under his wings
stop mid-song and freeze to a striding halt
when the coldest moment
hits the center of that night?
Or will he find his way
into the warm box of my house,
hide under the white acrylic bathtub,
tiptoeing out to play his song for me
as I sing along to my hallowed death,
rubbing chapped finger tips against each other,
round and round?

The Art of Instinct

Although everything always has everything to do with sex,

       each time, this one thing

has more to do with the sway of tree shadows

contained in rectangle boxes of light—

       reflections of the windows, yielding from the windows,

         caught in a breeze on the white plaster walls of the room—

and although it is often true the male of a species

has the more colorful markings, here I am the brightest one

       against the white sheets

          back arching,

a rising whale throwing its form from the sea

turning rose, then scarlet, then peony— light spreading across our flesh

       and the marvelous ability to be held by instinct.

The Art of Flight

These tiny Florida powderpost beetles
eat a little, fly a little,
then drop down and die.
Their flight, the smallest beating
of iridescent wings which my eyes can see.

I have a sadness
of not being a tree,
not being a landing place
for this kind of life.

Hottest Year on Record

I had a box full of pennies and nickels, a few dimes, from many years of putting change in a dish on the dresser, and then from the dish into a decorative box, and then from the decorative box into a children's shoe box. It was heavy, maybe 15 pounds. I took the box of money to Flamingo park and offered it to a man called Whitey who sat all day and night on a bench by the basketball courts. His eyeballs were in a constant flutter upward so only the whites of his eyes showed. But Whitey didn't want it. He shooed me away like a wasp. I carried the box of money a few blocks over and offered it to a woman who lives on the street, in an alcove next to the Bank of America. She was sitting up on her cardboard bed, rolling a cigarette, and said that it was too muggy to deal with a box of money. Across from the bank a guy had set up a card table and was selling two styles of tee shirts. One tee shirt was of a dog with pants on its back legs. The other tee shirt had the same dog but with pants on all four legs. The man said it was a famous question, to decide which you think is correct, a dog in pants with two legs, or a dog in pants with four legs. He offered to trade a tee shirt for the box of money, so I choose the dog with the pants on four legs. I went home and read about a storm that was coming in a few days which would cause the temperature of the North Pole to rise from 20 below zero to +35 degrees Fahrenheit, and then who knew what would happen with all the ice caps and glaciers and various frozen stuff that was holding our world in place. I sunk further into the soft beige foam cushions of my couch, taking no comfort from the cool air circulating around the room while my trouser-less dog panted in the famous heat.

Smash Shop

From the bench above the pond
I watch two ducks make dark channels
in the water as they feed,
pathways through a mosaic of cracked green ice.
Behind me the rocks, strata of red igneous beneath ochre sandstone,
are an unconformity— a geologic span—
characterized by an immense amount of nothing
between two calculable intervals of time.
Nothing not meaning that something wasn't there,
but that no thing remains
from the something that was.
I make lists of things here:
A female body is more regulated than weaponry;
white tigers swim like sharks onto flooded coastal streets;
this world might not be a mess
if individuals weren't imagining God.
My friend wants to create a Smash Shop—
a space where people can break as much as they want,
for as long as they like.
She envisions a warehouse full of junked cars
and thrift shop pottery,
long lines to get in,
because one of the things people do best
is destroy things.
The geologist Clarence Dutton coined the term
Great Unconformity, a concept indicating an absent interval
of geologic time.
In 1882 he couldn't date the rocks the way we can today,
still Dutton saw something was missing;
he just didn't know how vast it was.
My friend's idea is to have people pay by the hour,
but who will ever be able to stop?
The simple beauty of common things
makes us rage enough
to want to demolish everything in sight.

Bad, Bad Bodhisattva

Even though I vowed not to kill
I kill upward of 30 Key lime green caterpillars
that are eating my hibiscus hedge down to sticks.
This last one, before I stopped,
paused its eating,
lifted its mouth,
and turned its head toward the pressure of the scissors
as I was about to snip it in half.
I saw that it saw me
or felt me
and *knew* I was going to harm it,
but I killed it,
ashamed of my human nature
as it leads me,
clear-eyed,
into the snare.

Electrical Storm

When the lights went out
So many things were happening

But all I wanted to do was write a poem
About how good it felt

To fill buckets with cold water
From the gravity fed pump in the orchard

To walk across the tall summer grass
Feeling the hollow crush of deathlessness

Cushion the soles of my feet
And store the buckets under the porch

For drinking and safe keeping.
When the lights went out

The crickets strummed louder for mates
The stars shone brighter

A voice called out of the blackness
That was exactly me

Life is just a thing that feels like something.

When the lights went out
The canyon wren offered a feather to the night

And the bear shat in peace
Under the apple tree by the back door

It felt so good to be in the dark
With nothing turning on

And nothing turning off
To hear a voice that was exactly mine

And everything else's
At the same time

If you don't do another thing
You've done enough.

III

The nothing all wrens meant, the one feather on the road
—Larry Levis

Lay Hold of Me

Remember the giant whooping crane on the county highway
whose mate had been hit, stretched out dead at the center
of the road? She stood by him, wings open and flapping, shrewd
voice anxious, screaming, her dark red crown bowing in her descent
through the rim of despair. With each oncoming car she took a short
running flight to get out of the way, pacing the side of the road until
she could return to him. The next day, when still there, exhausted,
wings tattered and brown, we scraped what was left of her lover
off the asphalt with a snow shovel, and laid the body on the low,
dry threadgrass by the embankment. The birds had come that July
to our swale, which had filled with monsoon rain. She stood there,
close to us, in the still, yellowing grass, her interminable legs wobbling
underneath her body. The long toes of her feet twitching. That
shallow silver dish of my mind chattering, *lay hold of me. Lay hold.*

Osprey

This morning, waking from long
voluptuous sleep

I felt my life warm to this warming
world, and then fall away. The ledge

not crumbled beneath me
but pulled back,

as I stood at its edge.
Like that tablecloth trick

where the settings remain in place—

all my pieces intact as I fell
through the pine tops,

my mind loosening—
its language

the first to salute the velocity.

With my feet still on the granite
I looked up to see an osprey

flying just overhead,
a trout secure in its talons,

the fish's tail swimming through the wind.
I saw the yellow glint of its scales,

the flesh torn from a struggle,
then as if magic,

a drop of cool blood in my hair.

Basho,

When I get on a highway, and sometimes a mountain path,
I think about an accident which occurred years ago,
on the Long Island Expressway— a mother escaped her ruined vehicle
only to watch her young daughter's head roll across the 6 trafficked lanes,
coming to rest by a patch of daisies planted on the median.

When I learned of this horror, I thought of you, Basho,
and your poem, *Year after year on the monkey's face*
a monkey face.

Basho, when you say *Learn about pines from the pine,*
and about bamboo from the bamboo, I can do this.
When you are in Kyoto, longing for Kyoto
I am on my mountain, longing for my mountain—
walking among the things of this world that we call no world,
yet are, all the same, the world.

You say you are the hundred bones
and nine orifices of your body.
My one foot stands to the side of the other,
without any recognition.
The great horned owl, whose eyes stay fixed,
can turn its head 270 degrees
with the 14 tiny bones of its neck.

With you, Basho, I lie down
in the shade of a tree, and it knows us.
Together our heads roll with the wind,
are splattered with the rain.
Our eyes move with our necks.
Nothing is lost or used up.

Killing a Turkey at Belle's

Belle said I could have a turkey for Christmas if I killed it.
My children are in a field picking dried red chilies off frozen vines,
crushing them with their small fingers.
In the greenhouse we fill two sacks with the fresh basil
still growing up from the earth floor,
water what is left of the kale.
Soon it will all freeze.

Belle said it was easy to kill a turkey.
She would do one first and show me.
We walk to another field, closer to the river
and dig potatoes that will be cut up,
healed over for planting in the spring—
several pounds budding from each small seed piece,
a hand producing more fingers than it needs.

A muster of turkeys come racing up from the bosque
as if they were a litter of puppies and run toward the children,
that crimson skin on their necks bobbing like tongues.
The children run away from the turkeys,
who start to run away from them,
and then back again toward each other,
until my girl gets dizzy and slices her wrist on the barbed wire fence
she falls against to stop herself from falling.

I go back without the children to kill the turkey.
Belle watches me get out of my car as she finishes
scrubbing her kitchen window.
She was raised in a family of 10 children,
wants none of her own. The turkeys
are foraging in the dirt for kitchen scraps tossed
under the killing cones, which hang like lanterns on a rope
suspended between two ancient cottonwoods.

Belle comes out of the house with black mitts on her hands
carrying an iron caldron of scalding water in front of her.
She puts the water down by the trees,

grabs a turkey by its neck
flips it over so she's holding only its feet,
pushes its head through a cone, gives a tug at the neck,
then with one sweep of a machete,
its head falls to the ground.

Blood rushes out, a dam released,
pours copiously over the cold dirt, while steam
floats out from the head on the ground,
rises from the pool of blood.
Belle and I watch as the turkey's still beating heart
pumps all the fluid out of its body.
She takes the limp bird down, dunks it
in the hot water to soften it for plucking.

I can't do it.
The neckless bird is the shape of a swaddled
newborn baby. Belle says I should take the one she killed.
She will kill another one for herself.
She wraps it in newspaper,
puts it in a strong grocery bag with handles,
sets it in the back of my car.

We grab some blankets from the house,
walk through the yellow fields, down to the Rio Grande,
and sit on the bank throwing pebbles to her dog,
who curves his front paws into scythes
as he digs and digs in the shallow icy river,
below the freezing mud, reaping colored stones
from the barren water.

22

All that summer I marched braless around Manhattan
in a white tank top silk-screened with a seagull,
my nipples raising the tips of its wings toward the sky.
Auden was dead, but I swear I saw his ghost shuffling
along St. Mark's Place, in slippers, chewing on a piece
of Sicilian pizza. At home, across from Grace Church
we tossed our clothes in a pile on the floor, next to the
turntable which was propped on an orange milk crate
spinning non-stop with the tangy voice of Boy George.
None of us had bedroom doors, and at night
our private murmurs met like lovers in the shadowy
hallway. Poetry was something I knew I would never
figure out, but my body was handing over its secrets,
eagerly, and these pleasures continue unrivalled.

Mind-Blowing

Remember how huge I looked in that hideous melon colored dress,
the lavender lily print splattered on like giant food stains,

and how mind-blowing the sex was?
Every tissue inside me swollen to plum ripeness.

We outdid ourselves that first year,
two babies taking root—

it was as if a garden bed
had been raised inside me.

I felt so heavy with soil,
so tired from the constant tilling.

What a trick our bodies played on us:
there would be nothing carnal

about a child ruling our union,
but still the wanting—

so badly—

that sheer wet want of body on top of body,
the ends of my hair catching fire

as you leaned me over the stove
that last night we were alone.

Remember how her elbow
pushed through my abdomen like clay animation?

Then us, pushing it back,
until I felt the swim of her move up and under my stomach.

An oversized orange tee shirt was all I had on
as I labored her out of my body,

and at the end,
just when her crowning head was more out than in,

I pulled that shirt over my head
and threw it across the room.

Long Marriage

I have about 1000 postcard stamps, she says,
as his hand lifts her pajama shirt,

slides down her spine.
Oh, that feels good, she says, tucking a pillow between her legs, *can you rub this hip?*

I went to the post office yesterday and bought more by mistake, she says.
What? he says, pulling her closer, moving his hand across the small of her back.

And I cut my finger on the metal tab while closing the envelope I was mailing.
Look, she says, turning and placing her finger in his mouth.

Ooo, he says.
I organized all the stamps, by the way, she says.

I put them in one of those free parchment envelopes
with the postal service eagle head.

He slips his fingers lower, into her moistness.
Ummm, she says. *I've got to get up.*

Because they did it a few mornings last week,
he thinks they are going to do it every morning now.

That's good, she says, *but I've really got to get up.*
I need to make coffee.

Just relax, he says, kissing behind her ears,
shifting her shoulders and pressing her into the pillows.

She looks up at him, his eyes are wide open.
The loose skin on his face pulled down by gravity.

They are more sensitive now than when they were younger.
The membranes a little thinner,

their nerve endings more fine-tuned.

Vice Versa

I feel your sand
in our bed

and am at first
angry about this mess

but then I remember
your swimming legs in the sea

how they break at the knee
to kick away and then back

your long mind in agony
over what your body is doing

because you love the ocean
but dislike being in water

just as you desire me
but dislike the taste

of bitter greens
on your teeth.

Welcome

When I get to the hospital I see that someone has sent my grandmother a big bouquet of pink roses and the card reads: *Welcome.* Nana laughs and sticks the card on her morphine pump. She will only eat coffee ice cream with caramel sauce from Baskin and Robbins, which I run out to get for her from the shop on 66th and First. While she eats she tells me about her grandmother, Bertha Lauber, who was such a fanatic about dust that she stuffed tissue in the keyholes before leaving her beach house at the end of the summer. She also wrapped the phones in newspaper, and it had to be the issue from that morning, as it was the cleanest.

After 4 days of not moving her bowels, Nana moves her bowels, and everyone is very pleased. I tell her they put a sign on her door— *She Moved Her Bowels.* Nana laughs and then my uncle comes in and asks what all the commotion is about. Nana says, *Go read the sign.* They wheel her away for radiation. When she comes back all she says for the rest of the day is *Drip it up, sip it up.*

Are you used to being around Jews? Nana wants to know. *Ok, ok, I'll tell the story of how I met my Jew. He was not supposed to be drinking gin. We were only 16. I had long dark hair all the way down my back and my sister Patsy would braid it in twin strands and then coil it around my head as was the fashion at that time. Your grandfather came up to me at a party. He was already very drunk, and he said, "Why do you have that rope around your head? Do you think you are a challah?"* Nana is laughing so hard she bumps her face into mine. We look up and see Pop standing in the door, shy to enter the room. He is dressed up with a brown tweed vest under his suit coat and a light blue silk scarf folded in his chest pocket, but there is mustard crusted on his lapel. His gray hair sticks straight up, and Nana says, *O Bobby O Bobby O Bobby.*

When Nana leaves her room at the cancer center to go home, my uncle asks an attendant to donate the leftover cases of Ensure nutritional drink to other patients in the ward. While we are pulling away we see the attendant putting the cases of Ensure in the trunk of his car. Nana starts to laugh uncontrollably and the morphine drip dislodges from her arm, the liquid morphine leaking all over the front seat. She mops it up with a few tissues and squeezes the small amount of liquid onto her tongue.

Nana is in her bed, the twin bed on the right, which is pushed next to Pop's bed, the twin bed on the left. They are made up as they always are, with elegantly printed floral cotton sheets and the butter yellow monogramed blanket covers with white lace trim. She stopped talking a few days ago, and is flat on her back with her head propped up on two white pillows. Her face is an ashen blue. Pop puts on a freshly pressed pair of pajamas and goes to sleep next to her. I tuck myself into the seam between the two beds, like I used to do when I was a child, and rest a hand on Nana's chest, which is cornflower blue, and rises and falls weakly. She is so thin, each rib looks like a finger trying to poke through her papery skin. I place her fingertips in my hair and can almost feel them flutter like butterflies against my scalp. I lay my head on the small hill of her collarbone and imagine her tickling my back the way she's done all my life, with the smooth ends of her nails. I want to stay like this until she dies. I want to feel what happens to her body when her heartbeat stops, and then it does, and she dies. And her hands float up. And they graze my cheeks.

Sei,

On a night when you were waiting for someone to come
was this an empty time

or were you full of what the red mind makes?

Did you ever wonder about the first woman
who shaped her hand into a cup,

dipped it into a stream?
Did she drink the cool water,

or rinse her mouth of a pungent taste,
from the man she had taken in?

Men and women.
Two ways of thinking about the same thing.

In the day, I distinguish bird calls.
But with the evening, all desires sound the same.

The Way the Apples Sweeten

Underneath you, I don't move the way I once did.
It's not that I'm so ancient,
but enduring,
wiser now in these ways of body parts
and pleasure.
It's like apples on the tree in fall.
It depends on how the night hits them,
the way they sweeten.

Long Marriage

Have you come for happiness? He calls from a back room

while I am in the kitchen at the sink rinsing dishes.

Same as yesterday and the day before and the day before that.

How many times have I told him I can't talk, can't listen,
can't stop when the warm water is running through my fingers?

Can you sign this, he says, now at my side, *or can't you hear me?*

It is the same question, that as a boy, his father used to tease
   him with.

Do you walk to school or carry your lunch?

Departure

Rattle

Noticing the overhead kitchen light is on the blink,
she steadies her shaking wrist with her shaking hand,
spoons applesauce from the jar—
not much of a treat for her husband with 85 years
of good eating on his plate.
Not a comfort now, the soft sweet foods
served to him in a cut glass bowl
that had been in his own mother's home,
his mother having saved everything,
the silk and cotton dresses she had stitched by hand
and swaddled him in as a newborn.
Beige ribbon laced through the neck and waist,
kept by his wife in their own box,
passed on to their granddaughter,
who as a new mother did dress her daughter
in these delicately stained heirlooms.
She yells to her husband from the kitchen,
does he want a decaf?
No, he yells back, pushing his chair away from the table,
a loud scraping noise, and then a deep rattle,
a sound from the gut of a huge body of water,
and then a thud.
The ocean spilling onto the white linoleum tile.
Applesauce on the counter.
Applesauce on the floor.
The kitchen light blinking on and off.

Their Bodies

The pond at the end of the road.
The two scrubby pines by their door.
Nothing looks familiar when she comes home alone,
having left him on a single bed,
in a single room,

not able to move half his body,
or wanting to move the other half.
He has no more voice, but the words are there,
she can see the vast vocabulary in his eyes,
screaming that this should be over.
She should be widowed now.
After 64 years, he is ready to leave her body,
his own long legs having crossed each other for the last time.
She recalls when this was.
Yesterday before dinner they were having drinks on the deck, at sunset.
Their home built in the direction of the sunset for this purpose,
and as he looked out toward the ocean,
he crossed his right leg over his left,
sipped his white wine,
looked at his wife,
and was irritated that she hadn't fixed his dinner.
The phone rang then, but they didn't move to answer it.
These last months neither of them had been interested in anyone else,
each other's bodies the last points of departure.

    Om

They go to another city,
both of them disoriented now.
Some people try to get him to speak,
they try to get him to move.
All he can say is *Om*.
They think he is making progress, and will learn to talk all over again.
They try *Da Da Da* and *Ma Ma Ma*, but all he says is *Om. Om. Om.*
His daughters and his granddaughters and his great granddaughters
come to see him in his single bed, in his single room
filled with light and flowers and children's drawings,
and they can see he knows them,
but when they speak to him, he interrupts with his *Om, Om, Om.*
They bring him photographs of the water by his house,
of his younger self holding up a catch of fluke.
They bring him tapes they've made with soothing music.
He flails his one movable arm at them.

Gray foam collects in the corners of his mouth.
Dourly, he grunts along, *Om, Om, Om.*
They all know what he is saying,
but no one can take him there.

A Tiny Set of Claws

After a teeming rain, the beach packed firm, it is easy to walk on sand.

I look— I really look— into the eyes of each person who meets my gaze.
And I see— I can really see— that we look just alike.

Seagulls flock overhead, fight black beak to black beak
for a slice of yellow cheese someone tossed at them.

A fine-looking shell with a tiny set of claws inside
is washed in with the tide pooling around my feet.

On the way home, with a piece of driftwood, I scratch our initials
in the wet pink cement this city on the beach puts down for sidewalks.

29 years, U + Me
and still it feels as if we are getting away with something.

Suddenly; Rooted

Elder Ding can't stop bowing,
or throwing people off bridges as high as the Golden Gate.
He eats the word *suddenly* for breakfast,
and the word *rooted* for dinner,
or the other way around,
and spits out a koan of just these two words— *rooted; suddenly*
as if they were splintered chicken bones.

No matter where I stand,
I see hungry ghosts being freed from the bushes and from the grasses.
I recognize something in the wind—
when it reaches for me I go.

A friend tells a story of how he once chopped down a sixty-foot ponderosa,
which was in the way of his television reception.
When the blade of his saw hit the middle of the trunk the tree began to moan,
and then the tree shot a thick stream of liquid directly into one of his open eyes.
That tree, my friend says now, looking down at his hands,
it sprouted new feelers for years.

For Most of a Life

Everything narrows at the neck—
the infinite motion of a figure 8,
an old-fashioned glass egg timer.
The sifting through
of what is clearly uncertain: often
my breath gets stuck right there.
I place a hand over my heart and pull down,
pressing the ribs at the top of my chest,
to let the clutter out.

IV

Whatever such a mind sees is a flower,
and whatever such a mind dreams is the moon

—Basho

Here is a Pilgrim on a Waterless Shore

1

A month before spring,
the first day of spring arrives.
She cannot stop breathing in the scent of cold fresh water
where there isn't any water,
the smell of flowers
that haven't appeared.

She takes off her arms,
her legs,
unwinds her head,
tucks them into the compost with her breath.
Within minutes she sees the star-shaped leaves of the delphinium
stir under the mulch,
their shoots coiling around her wrists,
pulling her in.

A woman practicing for death
in the waking green undergrass of her life.
She has never lost an eye or a finger,
or even much bone.
She has not been splayed and sliced open,
arranged on a giant Styrofoam tray
by a man whose bathroom
is strung with human heads.

Now a buttery swallowtail lands on her arm,
the sleek black V at the end of its body a pulse
that offers her a shudder.
How possible it is to speak of something treasured
as we watch it appear.

An eagle is silent while circling its prey,
                as it pulls apart a rabbit under the moonlight
leaving the insides, leaving the white tail on the earth.

                The liquid bark of her runs down her throat,
                                out a hole at the bottom of a foot.

                It is the way of things to empty what is too full.
In a month, honeybees will drink from her neck,
                the plump yellow part of their bodies
                                hidden under furry black pollen from oriental poppies.

2

Each night a battle
                a wail
        one owl screeching from its same
and different self
        uuuuup uuuuup uuuuup.

Just after daybreak rain pours down from the sky in the distance
        as if it were lengths of long gray hair at the back of a woman's head,
                        while I am opening throat for muggy breath,
        facing forward into a sliding door that is not closed,
                waiting for the sky to shake its head over my little plot of comfort.

At the top of the ponderosa
        a gift of tail feathers,
                more orange-tipped than red-tailed hawk,
                                spiral down
        while in the garden a yellow breasted finch hooks feet
into the top of a finished sunflower head,

bobs for seeds as the sunflower head sways back and forth.

The finch's mate lands on her back,
jumps up and down as the flower head wrenches frantically,
                    forward and back, back and forward,
                                        loses his balance and quickly
        flies off,
            his little drip of seed seeping like a nap into the layers of her down.

How long does it take to wreck the good things we are given?
                        Not long, it turns out.
A dog dies in a few days without water,
we can go on longer,

        eat grass like a horse without throwing it up,
scratch in the dirt for grubs,
                    fold the giant gilded self in half like a piece of paper,
            and then into quarters,
            and then into eighths

all the time praying
                open, open,
                        another soft word for you will disintegrate anyway.

3

Sometimes when things come fast,
                        they are at their best,
        though you don't know this until later.

There are just twenty elements that make up who we are,
                        and if I were to list them all,
some of you would stop reading,

while others would go on with great interest.
Four elements are composed from the air and sixteen from the earth.

Like a stray dog, a dragonfly followed me home from the pond today,
and now he is circling overheard,
the extra-large size of this one casting dragonfly
shadows on the driveway like an aircraft.

If you were propelled into the center of the galaxy
and your sense of smell was still intact,
it would be familiar;
the scent of the universe is a raspberry and rum cocktail!

I would like to see the rare Cockerell bumblebees,
that have appeared in the White Mountains after 58 years.
If not in the tall pine forest,
then inside my breast.

I cannot explain the brown spotted moth
with the fin on its back like a shark,
or pale blue flowers blooming from sideways stalks,
stunning in their strange mutative quality.
The heat of the world feels good on my arms
as I hold them out for hours,
a dead branch in one hand—
a calmcrow,
a bird perch.
A black phoebe sidesteps almost to my wrist,
as I watch what is alone in this world turn into a ring of stones
around a single flowering desert daisy.

4

Do you know what's going on in there
                                deep down in the earth of the liver,
                    the canyons of the gut?

        This world,
                    our shores of gold
                                our mountains of red dirt—
        dust illuminates the light.

Early this morning, I couldn't help but touch the two mating earthworms
                                    as thick as my thumb.
        Entwined, the end of one pumping its juice
                        into the gonadal opening of the other.
But my finger ruined their ecstasy,
        and they sucked themselves back into their holes,
                                each one male and female,
each one soft and wide
                    from so much rain,
                    from so much sex.

It takes courage to be still,
            to wait in the dark for nothing.
                I pluck my hairs and shine my breasts,
sit in the center of the green spring lawn without moving a finger or a toe.

        The magpies shriek at each other
high above in the ancient cherry tree,
        a long married couple,
                        fighting over the few remaining cherries.
One of their blue feathers,
        dislodged in this squabble,
lands on my knee.

Most species on this planet don't even see us,
                                        or know we are here.
            And when they disappear
we easily find something else to hunt.

White fur from a rabbit's tail
            is caught in the splintery pine border of the vegetable bed,
                                        meaning the hawk has had its way again.

            I couldn't help but touch the mating earthworms.
                        This has to do with bliss,
which for me is the tips of my fingers on something more porous than myself.

5

I woke early this morning to the screams of a terrified cat
            as it was being pulled apart
                        by a pack of coyotes,
howling with glee as they wolfed it down.

The crickets, who had been up all night,
            were still rubbing their wings against each other,
                        exploding with want.

Later, on the nature hike,
            we are told that every part of the daylily is edible,
            and handed a freshly pulled petal to eat.
Some bees are territorial and nudge
            other bees away but they don't fight.

Some bees live in hives and work together,
            while others are solitary,
                        wall-papering their nests with the petals of flowers.

At the edge of the hummingbird feeder,
          which hangs from a thin crabapple branch,
a praying mantis lies in wait just above the spout,
                    attacks the next ruby throated
                                        that comes to drink,
wrapping its long front arms
          around the hummingbird's neck like two mini pythons.

          The bird whines like a puppy
as the praying mantis takes bites out of the flesh
from the side of its head.

The mantis would have eaten the entire hummingbird alive,
          as he batted his lime green wings futilely,
                    or died of a heart attack,
but the nature guide flicked the insect off the bird with his rolled-up hat.

In the copper birdbath,
          tiny hoverflies are sucking the head of a drowned white moth.
          I bend down close,
their shiny orange bodies almost to my lips.
                    We call it sky, I say to them,
                    but to itself it is an interminable beginning.

6

A hawk leaves the wet clay insides of its prey on the soil,
          also the nails of a foot,
                    a small rat's nose.

Here is a pilgrim on a waterless shore looking toward the ground for reflection.
          What rises up are the countless things
                    that have come together to produce this giant radish,
or a row of corn planted 18 inches into the earth.

To wake each day not knowing where I will go,
      returning,
                not knowing where I have been
                      is the prayer we each walk with.

Plea of hummingbird basket
    open sphere of moss and bits of lichen, every strand tucked in with precision,
a chalice growing out of the thin branch of a Russian olive,

brimming this morning with dew
                  wrung from a moonless night sky.

A common whitetail dragonfly
              his abdomen dipped in liquid chalk,
                    sunlight passing through the gossamer wings
            turns the black lattice work to orange,

a female on a dead pine branch warms herself in the sun
            is taken unaware by this aggressive male
their bodies curling into a heart
            as they stretch and bend toward instinct.

Above a black-chinned hummingbird flies in a horizontal line
                      the violet patina around his throat
shimmers as he dives toward the mating pair,
              snatches the male in his beak.

                  Busy with its own longing, a desert honeysuckle
stretches its vine toward the sun—
            its flaming petals shrivel in the heat
                as desire travels like lightening through the sandy loam—
but not into the blossoms and not into the air.

7

Ecstasy comes in lengthier moments now,
        comes when it's called,
and comes when it's not.

        A single thinning cloud disintegrating across this steely sphere of sky.
The one tree standing
        a little higher than the rest on the ridge of a mountain,
                in the distance.

Last night a clothes moth landed in my hair
        and laid her web of eggs close to my scalp.
                By morning, her body, a golden powder,
                        had spread across one of my eyelids like shadow.

Most of the time there is a non-linearity of things,
        but still I sense a line trying to draw me in,
                tempting me as if it were the snake charmer and I its curving form;
        but so curious to go against its nature,
                                so wanting to straighten out.

Here is a finger pushing itself into hot wax.
Here is a tongue putting its tip
        on a gritty stone.
Here is a sharp knife cutting ever so slightly
        into the thinnest part of a wrist.

What I continue to count on is flux;
        still, there are some things that do not move.

Every night a hawk. Every day,
        another set of rabbit innards
left behind on the ground.

I can't help myself,
　　　like a child
I find the nearest stick and turn them over,
the prize being a slithering nest of maggots,
　　　　　the flesh eaten through until the larvae on the bare grass become flies.

I thought it would be harder,
　　　　　to break the identity with the body,
　　　　　　　　with the mind,
but as it turns out, all I have to do is open my eyes,
　　　　　　　　　　　　and keep them empty.

8

The night the moon came for me she was not her usual womanly self,
　　　　　but rather a mannish intensity in a navy suit,
　　　　　　　　taking a firm grip on my wrist.
If you wake and come with me now, he said, *you will have a taste of what is enough.*

　　　　But I knew I would want more,
and then more:

　　　　That enigmatic joy of aloneness.

By the door, the red bucket was full of water,
　　　　　a black lizard filled the space with its swimming form.

At the edge of the yard a garter snake was giving birth.
　　　　The eggshells had dissolved in her body—
　　　　　　six writhing and wet licorice whip neonates emerged.

If you fall asleep curled around the hole of a black-tailed prairie dog
you will wake craving such broadleaf forbs as wild petunia, and sunflower.

If you fall asleep in a culvert under a narrow dirt highway
  your body will vanish by morning.

The night the moon came for me I was ready to go.
    I touched the long antennae of the pine sawyer,
and fed it drops of spit from my fingertip while it sat on the edge
    of the silver porch chair,
      a vagabond at rest.
Words, I told him, *are what I have been given to gnaw on,*
      but they aren't enough.
            They just are not enough.

So I open my mouth for timber and steel,
    and those jagged pieces of mountain that tumble down onto the road

                    and mark the way.

Refrain

Warm from the bed,
from the goose down,
I wake this morning
from the depths of not refusing
a long evening's sleep
accompanied by Whitman:
The curious sympathy one feels
when feeling with the hand
the naked meat of the body,
Whitman's body a refrain woven
through the red thread of me; a hard
freeze last night, and the light has changed
to the winter light.

Acknowledgments

Great appreciation to the editors of the following publications where these poems first appeared or were reprinted:

American Poetry Review: Lay Hold of Me, The Cows, Common Octopus, Which Yellow Bird, Ant Aubade

Crab Creek Review: Blue Reminds Me of the Truth

Hinchas de Poesia: 22, Mind-Blowing, Smash Shop

Indolent Books, What Rough Beast Series: Perfectly Made

JuxtaProse, Dear Basho,

On The Seawall: Killing a Turkey at Belle's

Orion Magazine: Next to You, Permanence

Miriam's Well: A Tiny Set of Claws

Monkey Mind: Marisela La Grave made On the Island of Koshima into a short video for Magnetic Laboratorium's online video poetry project

Ploughshares: Birds Eating Cherries from the Very Old Tree

Plume: "All the time I pray to Buddha I keep on killing mosquitos"

Poet Lore: Long Marriage (pg. 64)

Santa Fe Literary Review: The Art of Flight, Bad, Bad Bodhisattva

SoFloPoJo: Melancholia, Hottest Year on Record, Long Marriage (pg.58)

Taos Journal of Poetry: Blood Moon, Osprey, Basho, Refrain

The American Journal of Poetry: I Always Know Where to Put My Hands on a Tree, Curator of Insects, Here is a Pilgrim on a Waterless Shore

The Laurel Review: Here is a Pilgrim on a Waterless Shore (section 2), Mountains Hidden in Mountains, On Foot

The Miami Rail: Just Like That

Telepoem Booth: Birds Eating Cherries from the Very Old Tree, Dear Basho, and Lay Hold of Me were recorded for this project.

SWWIM: The Art of Instinct

Vox Populi: Birds Eating Cherries from the Very Old Tree, The Cows, Next to You, Permanence, Dear Basho, Which Yellow Bird, Welcome

WAVES: A Confluence of Women's Voices from AROHO: The Cows, Next to You, Permanence, Blood Moon and Smash Shop

Western Humanities Review: Stridulation

Women's Studies: An Interdisciplinary Journal: Welcome

Zocalo: Each Day Travelling

Many thanks to friends who helped with these poems and assembling this manuscript, especially Anne Marie Macari, Chase Twichell, Catherine Esposito Prescott, Joanne Dwyer, and Miriam Sagan. For his guidance and wise ways, for the brilliance of his own work, but mostly for the pleasure of his friendship, I am endlessly grateful to Tony Hoagland. Mountains of gratitude to everyone at Parlor Press, particularly Dave Blakesley for his stunning book design, support and kind patience, Jon Thompson for his thoughtfulness and for believing in this book, and Marianne Boruch for her generosity. Joanne Kaufman, my sister-in-law, is an amazing artist, and I thank her for the cover image, *Roses*. For time to write, I thank Herekeke Arts Center, Atlantic Center for the Arts, and Mabel Dodge Luhan House where I was the 2018 writer-in-residence. And then there is my family— David Kaufman, inexhaustible first and ongoing reader, partner in all joys and mishaps, and our children Willa and Oliver Kaufman— we begin together, again and again.

Dedications

Mountains Hidden in Mountains is for Roshi Joan Sutherland

Violets is for Martha Abatuno

On Foot is for Tony Hoagland

Common Octopus is for Roshi Joan Halifax

Just Like That is for Tony Hoagland

Smash Shop is for Kira Jones

Killing a Turkey at Belle's is for Willa Kaufman and Oliver Kaufman

Welcome is for Jean and Robert Jacobson, and Arthur Jacobson Sr.

Departure is for Pauline and Richard Kaltenbacher, and Nancy Strauss

A Tiny Set of Claws is for David Kaufman

Suddenly; Rooted is for Frederick Turner and Patricia O'Hara

Here is a Pilgrim on a Waterless Shore is for New Mexico

Notes

1. *Not into the Blossoms and Not into the Air* is from Larry Levis' poem *Threshold of the Oblivious Blossoming* in his book *The Darkening Trapeze*.

2. *The Cows* references a story by Lydia Davis from her book *can't and won't*.

3. *Mountains Hidden in Mountains* is from Mountains and Waters Sutra by Eihei Dogen, translated by Kazuaki Tanahashi

4. *Blood Moon* remembers Matthew Shepard, December 1, 1976 – October 12, 1998

5. *I went out following the scented grasses, and returned chasing the falling blossoms* is a koan by Changsha translated from the Chinese by Joan Sutherland.

6. Japanese Haiku Poets:

   Matsuo Basho – 1644-1694
   Yosa Buson – 1716-1784
   Kobayashi Issa – 1763-1828

7. *Sei Shonagon – 966-1025* is the author of *The Pillow Book*

8. *The curious sympathy one feels when feeling with the hand the naked meat of the body,* is from Walt Whitman's *I Sing the Body Electric*.

DATE DUE JUL 11 2019

PRINTED IN U.S.A.

90

About the Author

ELIZABETH JACOBSON is also the author of *Her Knees Pulled In* (Tres Chicas Books) and two chapbooks, *Are the Children Make Believe?* and *A Brown Stone* (dancing girl press). She is the founding director of the WingSpan Poetry Project, a not-for-profit which conducts poetry classes in community shelters in Santa Fe, New Mexico. Her work has appeared in the *American Poetry Review, Poet Lore, Orion Magazine, Ploughshares, Plume, Taos Journal of Poetry, The American Journal of Poetry, Terrain, The Miami Rail, Vox Populi,* and other literary journals. She has an MFA from Columbia University.

Photograph of the author by Arthur Jacobson. Used by permission.

Free Verse Editions

Edited by Jon Thompson